Einstein's Bicycle

A cycle ride through Eliot's Waste Land

Terry Dammery

Einstein's Bicycle

Published by The Conrad Press in the United Kingdom 2020

Tel: +44(0)1227 472 874
www.theconradpress.com
info@theconradpress.com

ISBN 978-1-913567-17-0

Typesetting and Cover Design by: Charlotte Mouncey, www.bookstyle.co.uk
The Conrad Press logo was designed by Maria Priestley.

Printed and bound in Great Britain by Clays Ltd, Elcograf S.p.A.

Life is like riding a bicycle.
To keep your balance,
you must keep moving.

Albert Einstein.
Letter to his son, Eduard, February 1930

The Preface

My mother died and I thought of how awful things had been. So, I sat down and wrote the first draft of Einstein's Bicycle. It was difficult at first because, even though I had spent a lifetime thinking of her, I hadn't seen or heard of her in over sixty years, going as she did to Australia when I was still a schoolboy.

It was only by chance that I learned of her death and how she had been buried in a Melbourne cemetery – the young, teen-aged mother I knew as my sister had grown old and died half a world away.

She was an Islington girl, born in 1922, the year that Einstein's theory of relativity was proven and the year that Eliot's *The Waste Land* was published. This latter coincidence cast my mother and my grandmother as two of Eliot's vulgar London women, morally decadent like others of their class.

In this role they experienced the remembrance of a wasteland along the Western Front, the General Strike, the breadlines and soup kitchens of the thirties and the declaration of another war. It was into this particular wasteland that I was born.

There was nothing unique about our position. We were part of a long historical line that stretched back as far as Chaucer – noble antecedents but far from nobility. We exemplified Eliot's low-brow, invidiously contrasted with his own high-brow – he and his Bloomsbury set exemplifying the establishment.

Ostensibly, *Einstein's Bicycle* is about the travails of a mother and her child through difficult times, but it was only during proof reading that I realised what it was really about.

In the past, I had written a doctoral thesis on a philosopher who argued that the establishment achieves compliance through ideological and cultural means – hence subjugation is just an accepted fact of life.

I'd felt that those thoughts were long buried but, like Eliot's corpse, they'd resurfaced in the text of *Einstein's Bicycle* which seems to grudgingly document the successful working of what is now known as 'cultural hegemony'.

Eliot was well placed to play a significant part in that process. With his hierarchical view of culture, his position in publishing and his affinity with the Bloomsbury set he was able to shape contemporary taste and culture for decades.

Thus, *Einstein's Bicycle* can be seen as an implicit cultural critique of Eliot with *The Waste Land* viewed as the product and exemplification of establishment perspectives and cultural values. However, the poem, *Einstein's Bicycle*, was written as a biographical narrative and not literary criticism - *The Waste Land* a conveyance, not the subject of analysis.

Literature's sway is part of a pervasive and subtle didactic, seemingly as benign as our mothers' milk, but did no more than give me an antithetical stance on life, which it seems I have never lost. And so, while *Einstein's Bicycle* is far from being a socialist tract, it is unashamedly prejudicial – you can only speak, only write, from where you stand.

Hence, while *Einstein's Bicycle*, the poem, the book, is the celebration of a culture as old as Chaucer, it is also the outpouring of sixty and more years of secretly nursed emotion and resentment, that pulls together many, many scattered moments of reflection.

Terry Dammery May 2020

The Prologue

Like a poet or a painter, what we know of life,

the clouded truths of metaphor,

the vibrancy of the vernacular, depends on where we stand.

Our baggage,

bundles of cultural legacies,

define the difference

between those who view life's drama,

life's pilgrimage,

seated in the galleries

and those who see it standing in the paupers' pit.

Most tales are told from the galleries

but some, like hers, theirs,

they come from below.

A child herself, she bore another,

shadows of the Cenotaph, long across a wasteland.

Their tale trailed centuries, clichés of a class,

fields to factories,

waiting, needing to be told, a conveyance

for the telling of carefully buried truths.

But like the villain in a pantomime,

there came, imperiously,

like a god from the slopes of Mount Olympus,

an unheroic Grecian hero,

sailing over oceans, to steal the golden fleece,

to give a tall-told tale of fiction, the authority of truth.

The audience, aloof in the galleries, loved it,

applauded its lofty tones,

standing ovations,

relief maybe, when really

all they understood was that it didn't vulgarise them.

The groundlings, standing belittled below,

they knew better,

how you can only talk from where you stand

and how they'd witnessed,

stood impatiently through,

a travesty,

a fabrication,

a misreading of national grief as cultural decadence.

They'd paid their pennies,

it seemed, just to watch the pigeons fly the yard.

But they'd seen tragedy, comedy and history,

knew them all

and thought of fields too long laid fallow.

Offspring, proud, of bowmen they were,

wearing with pride, the wounds won on Crispin's Day.

And so,

thinking to usurp the stage,

they turned and raised two fingers to the galleries.

The Tale

The blood of centuries runs through our veins,

age calcifies our bones

and the waters of the Thames flow sweetly through our thoughts.

We walked the ways with Chaucer, rehearsed our tales

over jugs of ale, close at the Tabard Inn

and

come tragedy or comedy, we stood crowded in the paupers' pit.

Runnymede meant nothing to us,

knowing it was our longbows that felled the knights.

We held our silence, never said a word, didn't ask for more,

but never did forget to keep our bowstrings waxed.

Children of the fields, descendants of the levellers,

we came in off the land,

to cities and factories, mined coal and worked the looms.

We saw the train overtake the barge,

the car pass the horse and the bus replace the cart.

There'd been plagues and there'd been fire,

wars and subjugation,

but integrity is the one prize we've never, ever lost.

We are the foot-soldiers, bowmen,

women chained to railings,

time's pilgrims, all of us, honing our knives quietly as we go.

*

Some of us missed the first performance

but arrived in good time for the second.

10

Like buses down Whitehall,

you wait a century and two come along at once.

There were no bells,

the lights down low,

barges hooting along the river, below the tidal reach,

and the water wide on the flood, mud-banks on the ebb.

When the second came along we began to number them

and the Great became the First,

the last,

the one before,

shifting sadly into the wings.

And the present, it took centre stage

as we, in the paupers' pit,

listened to the sirens wail and made ourselves ready,

anxiously,

for the 'repel borders' scene, muskets from the fighting tops.

Every night they came,

the raiders,

regular as the tides that swelled the docks,

following the river, shining silver, inland from the coast,

the moon, bright as sixpence in the sky.

Then would come the fireworks,

incendiaries to set the night on fire,

whistling as they fell.

But we were tired of tragedies,

had seen them all before, our faces hung in grief.

*

Lutyens, though, after the armistice of the First,

had built a cenotaph, lest anyone forget

and let us read our history through a nation's eyes,

opening the gates of mercy, revealing the conscious truth.

Carved from Portland stone, it was,

sarcophagus and all,

twice the height and more of every London bus,

yet too small to hold the names of all that we had lost.

*

For too long there'd been talk of officers and men,

soldiers and generals,

field hospitals and trenches,

of telegrams read on doorsteps.

Time to say good-bye to all that, or so we thought.

Sad couplets, it seems, never disappear,

they just take another form.

In twenty-two, there came Ulysses and Doctor Dolittle,

the Silver Ghost and the Austin Seven,

no spirit of ecstasy for most of us

and later, of course,

the First World War became the Second World War.

That same year, of twenty-two, Hermann died,

he so clumsy with his ink.

While in October Marie stopped following her van.

And Eliot, too self-absorbed to care,

built a pedestal in honour of himself,

taller than the Cenotaph, just a trace of Chanticleer.

A literary collage, he gave us,

indelicately called The Waste Land, mindful of the gap.

The chattering classes loved it, or laid claim to,

chewed its fragments over dinner,

but we, the hoi polloi, were busy grieving for the dead,

a country,

a people convalescing,

recovering from the horrors of the fight.

Call it moral decadence, which he did,

a cultural waste land, if you like, but it's far from being the same.

Lutyens knew the difference,

and let the bereaved recognise themselves,

saw us huddled in our grief, the flu around our doors,

waiting,

patiently and blameless,

for the sweet-smelling showers of April

to quench the drought of March.

Meanwhile, along the road in Islington a baby cried,

Wednesday's child, full of woe,

maternal infanticide debated in the House,

an innocent in Eliot's waste land, winter stretching in to spring.

Yes, twenty-two was a very busy year,

although Carter,

Lord Carnarvon's man,

found time to open Tutankhamen's tomb

in the Valley of the Kings,

more gold,

more beauty than the bullion, sterile in Fort Knox,

and his, the first breath,

the first footfall in three thousand years of dust.

But the prize that year, the year of twenty-two,

Eliot up-staged,

eclipsed even,

went to a self-effacing patents' clerk,

his brain the size of a planet,

who gave us the poetry of space, the subtleties of time,

unpretentious

on the humble bicycle he took each day to work,

the simple lesson it had for life.

*

Versailles, it seems, had squeezed the pips,

hunger was the problem,

not moral turpitude,

but over the water, guns before butter the clear priority.

And so, the class of forty, heard crying in the wings,

became the players, their parts on centre stage,

as mothers wept,

like the families of the first,

knowing as they would,

how no-one there is, ever replaces any-one that was.

And the cold wind blew

as the months came cruel as April does

while we,

in the long shadow of the cenotaph,

were left waiting to know our names

and for them to be etched on every village stone.

Down along the busy high-streets

where carts had gone to cars,

each moment was the focus, whatever helps will do.

Trolley-bus booms swished on the bends,

milk on every door-step, tops popping in the frost,

and coal smoke

rising grey from soot-black stacks, curling in cold winter skies.

*

Summer, still she comes

and Wednesday's child pretty as a picture

steps gentle through the heady days of June.

Cycling lightly, her dress floating,

19

she drifts, legs pale, down the empty side roads

and ambles aimlessly across the poet's waste land,

not so very far from school.

And he, he was much older than before,

her mother's bed still warm,

a rude mechanical, a family friend,

face carbuncled, much like an ass and her too young to know.

Naivety, virginity,

like the flags in shreds along Whitehall,

decreed by fate, maybe,

a dislocation of what should have been, perhaps,

but exploitation, not so very far from rape.

A loveless moment,

viewed naturalistically,

the way life is,

he no Romeo, she no Juliet,

but, takes two it seems and innocence absolutely no defence.

*

To the hop fields with her sister, they go with Sally Ann,

Bermondsey and Bethnal Green,

discreetly filling time,

the baskets heavy, pulling on the bines.

A miscarriage maybe, to bring it off perhaps

as fighters tangle in a clear, blue summer sky,

where youth, not so very far from school,

ride the screaming Merlins, astride the rattling cannon.

Deflection shots and barrel rolls, chasing for the kill,

all to keep the initiative,

trying to stay alive.

And she, well,

their burden so much heavier, her dilemma nothing like.

*

So much to lose, a bird with broken wings,

but sepsis, haemorrhage, oh la de dah,

infections,

damage to the genital tract,

the mother's life, maybe, and certainly another's.

Eighteen is when the soldiers die, their names on village stones,

so just lie back and push for England,

why don't you

and let the little bastard live, quid pro quo and all.

Just let it be, let it be, but she not old enough to know

and things too soon to show,

how there's no need to be enthralled,

no need to live in fear of fate, of nature's laissez-faire.

Later she'll see the buddleia grow,

tall from the arid mortar dust, racemes of powder blue,

filling the bombsites with butterflies,

red admirals, tortoiseshells and peacocks,

explosions of beauty, splendour from the rubble of a blast.

And she will learn, too, how love lies bleeding

in the pavement cracks,

the gaps where the sun shines through,

23

where once the buildings were,

gone,

unplugged, extracted

like pulled teeth, in the pain, in the tooth-ache of the raids.

So let it be, let it be,

nature will give the answer, let it be, let it be.

*

But –

a glass of porter in a Lambeth pub, a tube away from Islington,

an apron stained beneath her coat,

a woman with a homely smile,

a friend of a friend,

of a friend of a friend,

names laundered as they go so only sinners,

it seems,

see eye to eye, the face, the door that fronts the crime.

You can go up west, but it'll certainly cost you more,

it's cash up front she takes. Well,

it's a risk for both sides, dearie, I'm sure you'll know,

she's done a lot, though,

and I'd trust her with my life.

She don't advertise, luv, you'll understand,

but a nice front parlour

with lavender polish and no ash in her clean black grate.

Circumspection behind a knitted brow.

So strange,

how does she know it all so well,

with her hair that smells of cooking.

*

Decisions and revisions which a minute will reverse,

but Queen Mab,

she lives up west in Kensington,

a step or two, and more, from Islington,

so she can't afford the cost to be given back her wings.

Fate's fawning fingers, ambiguous gifts,

undesired yet unreproved,

just as sweets taken from a stranger

always demand a forfeit.

But the thread is spun, for both of them

as her train clicks north, over the points, sweating with the load.

Gone by winter fields, ploughed for spring,

through thickets where wanwood leafmeal lie,

so still in the frost-filled air.

A cold coming it was, just the worst time of the year,

the ways deep and the weather sharp,

yes, a cold, cold coming she had and, for her, so early too.

*

Like trackside telegraph poles, their looping wires,

life's little couplets, black and white,

north and south, war and peace,

maids and matrons, of honour or not,

she knew them all.

But what of her and Hardy's Tess,

Eliot's careless typist suffering exploring hands,

the kick of life in a young girl's womb, a beginning or an end.

And the wires, they still looped along beside the track,

hypnotic as a pendulum swing, a thurible maybe,

but no demure altar boy,

no sweet scent of innocence, just coal

and a snake, maybe, a sated serpent sliding along the banks.

Whatever the wires, there was no doubt,

it was the leaving of Goldengrove,

the blight she was born for,

her grief for no-one but herself.

And, there was no parsley, sage, rosemary or thyme,

no midsummer night's dream and she no duped Titania.

The north, it was another country, she another person,

Lowry's factories,

pit-ponies grazing in the frosted fields,

silvered roofs,

sparkling pavements,

the quiet bliss of each passing day,

and the beauty, the brittle cold

of the star-bright nights, blessed with hymns and carols.

But winter strips the bark, silver from the birch,

crops, golden from the fields,

a north-east wind

blows up the Tyne, cold on the face of southern girl,

the sheep in huddles beneath the drystone walls

and so, what does the robin do then,

poor thing,

a wing,

a prayer in an abbey porch, the worst of winter yet to blow.

*

There was no-one pacing anxious in a waiting room,

or flowers by a bed,

just the screams of birth and a ticket back down south.

Less import than a mason's mark on an abbey stone,

far from the poet's romantic vision

and no truth, no heaven that lies about us in our infancy.

Reality,

it's clear, is much more stark,

just the same old loops of track-side wires

and the clack of the wheels on a southern train,

trailing no clouds of glory, just steam, smoke, grit and smuts,

to the tune of a mewling child that won't be fed.

*

The priest, oh the priest, he slurs his words,

nose red as altar wine,

can't show it in the pews, you know,

distraction from their prayers, especially if it cries

and how will you feed it.

I mean we can't have that,

there's no room for prams either, not as though it's Christmas.

And there is a war on, which of course you'll understand.

It'll have to be adopted, exported maybe, even,

then you'll have your freedom,

but of course, well,

you'll always carry the guilt, heavy as any growing child.

Moral as a maiden aunt, comforting as tooth-ache,

rehearsing a self-righteous text,

the message of the judgement mural in every mediaeval church.

And always he smiles, teeth yellow as his fingers,

so secure

always certain

no-one ever draws the shortest straw,

yellow teeth, yellow fingers,

same apologetic tone, same softly spoken strictures,

regular as a rocking horse, the letter not the spirit.

What does he think when he spills the altar wine,

all that he doesn't drink,

safe in his pitch-pine shelter

only seeing what he wants.

But Sally Ann,

she understands, seems it's the singer not the song.

*

Splintered timbers, floorboards for a fire,

a woody smoked to calm

and food, food from Sally Ann.

Just let the little bastard sleep, better for both if he did

and she, well,

her child too young to be an orphan.

Regular as a beating heart, the wailing of a siren,

they came each night again,

the Dornier.

Their throbbing,

their droning, moaning and humming,

the grim verse of assonance, even the deaf can hear.

There's a cupboard under the stairs,

black as coal, like the soot around the stacks,

up where search-lights slice the dark, piercing the night,

holes in the heavens

where flames lick the stars,

chaotic, anarchic, no-one, nothing to stem the flow,

excessive,

unedited like an autocratic text,

blood streaming in the firmament.

The whole of eternity, and perdition by a fluke of fate,

and yet,

come phlegm, flu, bombs and gripe,

like the buddleia from the rubble,

butterflies and love lies bleeding,

seems clay still grows tall, in spite of everything and all.

*

Take him down the tube, luvvy, it's warmer there,

safer too.

Jerry can't get you there.

You can't live in boarded basements,

out of a coal-house pram,

what about your mother, can't she help you out.

You could, of course, give your child to us,

visit him when you like.

You decide, we'll help you till you do,

but nights, luvvy,

you take him down for shelter,

it's warm, no-one'll mind, and it's almost fun,

the songs and all.

You'd be surprised the things they do down there.

But if you're worried, go to a station along the line,

they'll not know you there

and you'll get the sympathy you and he deserve.

It looks as though you need it, both of you.

*

With her guilt curled sleepy on a blanket at her feet,

beneath the switch-board where she works,

smelling the leather of her shoes,

she pulls the plug on the way things are, ending a nuisance call.

Like a heavy sack emptied down a coal-hole chute,

all and everything excused

swallowed in the black-out

a dog put down,

left abandoned in the ruins, the disposal of a body

and she left crying at the dark end of the tube.

Separation more acceptable than termination,

abandonment

the better side of infanticide.

Hetty left hers in a field,

poor Fanny took hers to the grave

and the cold stare of opinion,

ugly as the gargoyles that keep the weather from the fabric.

Sisters of Charity, the nuns of St Vincent,

everyone knows they take them all,

an assembly hall behind a tall brick wall,

the mannered convent girls gone safely to the shires.

Rows of beds,

beads, crosses, and high starched hats,

the smell of urine and carbolic, incense of the times.

No name and no possessions,

no clutter, no past,

no soft toys or bears

and nothing, not ever, the same again.

Sally Ann, she gives no sermon,

knows it all, done it all before and carries her loads for free.

See the soldiers laid in rows, always them,

always they,

and you have to get so close to find they have a name,

each one a person,

every one a mother's child.

It's how crowds are formed, aggregates piled,

the rubble of the pavements,

when pronouns replace the names, colour blurred to grey.

It's the way a he, a she, becomes a we,

a them versus an us,

like the poet's stereotypes,

labels and devices that allow the creation of a waste land.

*

But we are gristle, sinew, we are bone

and we never shed a tear,

our eyes fixed in an ever vacant stare

so we never have to talk and never be a friend

and we never ever use our names,

quietly, we rock ourselves to sleep each night,

hoping, strangely, for the dawn.

We know about the dormant days of winter,

of life held in parentheses,

but we know nothing of cultural decadence

and none of us

ever needs the strictures of a puritanical mind,

we're just too busy surviving the privations of our being.

And so, we sleep every night with open eyes,

waiting, maybe, for Chaucer's spring,

knowing, listening from our beds, how the world will end,

how death will come

like a thief in the night,

a floating warhead falling quietly through the dark,

filling the silence,

those empty moments between the buzz and the bang.

And we, poor bare-forked things,

left charred,

like the ember-black gibbet trees from the one there was before.

*

They lived in London, all of them, grandmother, mother

and her sister,

the reason he was there, under the flight path of the Dornier,

the trajectory of the rockets,

his family housed close by.

But in all the time, like Eliot and his Vivienne,

they never came, no, they never came to visit.

How was it they slept at nights, talked

and fed themselves,

with skeletons swinging, rattling in every cupboard,

the cold draft of guilt billowing their blinds,

guttering candles,

blowing through their consciences,

filling every silence.

And he

hardly knowing who he was, forgetting who they were.

She, though, moved out of London,

took a train to the coast, the minute the rockets fell,

while her mother and her sister, they moved up west,

safer there, then all the way to Cornwall,

to a house that was sweet and twee,

with a chamomile lawn, maybe,

and no rubble,

slates or broken glass heaped in mounds along the paths.

Perhaps, just possibly, Eliot had things right,

or better, maybe,

Einstein's law of bicycling is what it was really all about.

And Eliot, what of him? Well,

he became an air-raid warden, to expiate his arrogance,

temper his aloofness,

maybe get to know the people,

a case of Tom and not TS, a pair of overalls for work.

*

While Eliot, in fancy dress, walked the blacked-out streets

and Vera, with the head-scarfed mill girls,

cycled dutifully to work,

affluence wobbled and sold its soul.

Poets, playwrights, diplomats and celebrities,

Oxon, Harvard and the like,

migrated,

patricians in a panic, gone to sunnier climes,

commoners left pumping up their tyres, for the onset of winter.

And it's altogether now,

Wish me luck as you wave me goodbye.

Cheerio, here I go, on my way.

Such a pity about the passport and the laureate,

the butt of sack, the egg on an ambassador's face,

but there'll be a cosy cottage and a very comfy chair

when a class forgives itself.

*

44

Four hundred oil-lamps lit the castle of a duke,

things of beauty, like the treasures that they light,

stretching days into nights,

winter into spring, bright as the gold

buried in an Egyptian crypt, so it's jolly dee for the duke.

The black-out should have made us equal

but our hurricanes they flicker in the draft

that blows below the stairs,

through sacks filled with spiders,

a century's worth of dust

where our candles, they gutter,

throwing shadows, leering, sneering on the walls,

never burning at both ends, they have to last the night.

We sit chilled in the stone-cold safety of the cellars,

the gloom of some walled-up tomb,

waiting while Carter comes to find us,

to be his 'wonderful things',

after all, we too were young, just not kings, dukes or earls,

but we were alive

and we sang about the rich man in his castle,

the poor man at his gate,

how beauty, it lies everywhere, if there's light enough to see.

All things bright and beautiful,

the death mask of a pharaoh,

the polished oil-lamps of a duke,

the Lord God made them all,

but,

those of us he left down by the gate,

sadly,

missed out on the light, the bright, the beauty and all.

It's a long, long way from Merton, Camden Art College,

from Trinity too,

or a commission in the London Welsh.

Poor Private Jones, just a foot soldier

so no-one seemed to notice he hadn't been killed

in that mess-up on the Somme, all those years before.

Ask him, John Ball and Dai Greatcoat,

they'll tell you about a wasteland, that first long day,

with their musket, fife and drum,

wresting Mametz Wood from the rattle of the gun.

Three years in Rats Alley they were,

Private Jones and all,

where the dead men really did leave their bones,

scattered along the lines of a poem

that tells of killing fields

with mud, rats and the sniper's gun,

but no indulgences or shameful appropriations

and no obsessive trivia about broken fingernails or dirty hands.

Like us, they'd drawn their bows at Crécy, at Poitiers

and our arrows flew with theirs at Agincourt,

quicker than a crossbow, unseating the imperious French knights.

We were Shakespeare's archers in Henry Five,

heroes of St Crispin's day,

yet left by the generals, guilty of a country's blood,

not to reason why, but to do and die,

to fight a variant of the Maxim with a variant of the pike.

And we, we always presume our turn, detritus of the next

and think as we did before,

day by day in our wasteland,

of the sudden violences and the long, long stillnesses.

*

We have parts in a dystopia we're not meant to grasp,

like children who think with broken images.

But all of us,

we know that no-one likes a clever-dick

and anyway,

we're more than slugs and snails and puppy dogs' tails.

Listed in Froissart, we stand taller than the knights,

pedigree enough to carry a library of English classics.

We are the Bard's Falconbridge, Fielding's Tom,

Emily's Heathcliff,

Eliza and Harriet in the pages of Jane Austen.

We are everywhere in Dickens and the Elegy is ours.

Beware of us, for we are Prospero with his magic,

Wyndham's cuckoos before the tale was told,

children of rapes, survivors of miscarriage,

self-induced and fudged.

And we are golden-eyed and telepathic,

we can crumble walls

and read men's minds, like Rorschach with his ink blots.

Sadly, we are anathemata,

like the soldiers at the front, sacrifices to your gods,

a title appropriated

dug up, vandalised, from the wasteland where we died.

Sneer at us, dismiss us at your peril,

for we'll be your conscience the minute you reflect,

that all the pennies in a collection box

will do nothing to assuage

and know that we'll not, never let you quite forget.

For we will fill the silence of our forebears,

who lie without, in the churchyard of St Giles.

We'll be the ghosts of the fallen,

of the mothers,

of the children,

the Eumenides, the furies that come snapping at your heels.

*

The East End heard it first,

the drone of the Dornier following the moonlit river,

and, even before the sirens, ducked low before the blast,

beside the wharfs along the docks,

the jagged warehouse blocks.

They heard the whistle of incendiary sticks,

the crackle of burning timber,

saw flames that light the night,

and we,

distracted in our cellar, sing London's burning,

London's burning,

fire fire, fire fire,

pour water, pour water,

fetch the engine, fetch the engine.

London's burning, London's burning,

with all the mannered convent girls

gone safely to the shires

and we,

grateful for the spaces that they left, too hazardous to be.

*

A smell of ammonia fills the hall,

the sheets pulled back,

drying for the night,

survivors of the backstreets, fatalities of the fight,

trying to see the light

through black-blinded windows, the beds aligned in rows.

Come war or come the peace, it's all the same,

prisoners that carry no crime,

patients who suffer no sickness,

just vacant stares,

emotional voids, no laughter, warmth or tears,

lobotomised,

cauterised, babies for the maidens that have no crying.

Wards, cells, asylums, call them what you like,

dotted along the flight-path, below where the rockets buzz,

where one goes east,

one goes west

and one flies over the cuckoo's nest.

Outside the gates, a wasteland beyond the yard

streets like lines of broken teeth,

boarded houses,

the families all flown,

just sparrows in the spouts,

more value than a ration book,

worthless coupons in empty shops, walls of empty shelves.

But He knows, we're told, of every sparrow that falls,

of all the cancelled ration books,

every boarded shop,

the stumps of all the houses gone

and we,

thinking as we listen, of the cow that jumps over the moon.

*

Blinded by the black-out,

we see the shrimp girl in our heads,

now there's flesh and blood for you,

we hear the widow say.

And we feel in the instant

a deep respect for Hogarth, his paintings and his politics.

A Londoner to his toes, he knew his subjects well,

the iniquities of his time,

profligate, indulgent and complacent,

his maiden to a harlot, her innocence exploited.

Edgy and reformist,

he saw Londoners as close as Chaucer

and knew it all first hand, his father interred in Fleet.

Buried in a Chiswick church-yard, an epitaph from Garrick

who summarised it all,

how his paintings

reached the noblest point of art, a laureate before Nobel.

Booth picked up the challenge, explicit in the artist's work

and gave us Sally Ann.

While Dickens, a father too in prison,

wrote his way to Poets' Corner for taking up the cudgels,

letting Oliver tell our story, focussing

the footlights on those of us buried in the paupers' pit.

But the ugly social truth, torn from his novels,

blows, swirling in the alleys,

clichés that litter a waste land in a poet's derivative script.

Chaucer and Hogarth, Booth and Dickens,

kindred spirits all, and then along comes Eliot,

lofty and aloof,

the bloodiest snob, as Vivienne said.

She, Skinny Lizzy from Ash Can Alley

and he Lord Snooty, knowing nothing of who we are,

gloved like royalty,

for fear, God forbid, he should ever have to shake our hands.

*

She was guiltless, she was blameless,

footloose and fancy free,

V1's buzzing in the London skies,

troops lying dead on Normandy beaches

and she marries, yes, she marries,

her dodgy past just a stiff, laid cold in a war hospital bed

and her child safely locked away

in the silence of her thoughts, behind some convent walls.

There was no conscience that troubled her,

no North Atlantic convoy, no enemy coast ahead,

no,

not a worry in her head, phased by nothing, Hitler at her door.

When the end is near, seems you make the most of what there is,

let the bombs fall

and the shelters fill.

Nero fiddled as Rome burned,

Drake bowled as the Armada sailed.

And why not for her,

what difference hedonism, methodism, a blanket or a shroud.

*

Like monks in a Carthusian monastery,

we live a life that's mostly inside our heads,

expressionless faces,

staring eyes,

our thoughts never betrayed,

secure,

always hidden,

behind our bricked-up walls.

We might be hearing our mothers scream,

the crackling, dying breath of a father in the dry desert sand,

but we don't flinch a muscle,

never shed a tear

and like brothers adhering to a vow, we never say a word,

holding our monastic silence, until someone calls our name.

*

We were blown before the blast, shrapnel

in the wind,

left waiting for the flood,

the breaking waters of the Tyne,

moonlight silver on the Thames,

where the hollowed stems of the river's reeds

lie broken by the towpath, below the tidal reach,

below the bankside stumps of splintered trees.

We are the lost souls, left like litter,

dropped handkerchiefs,

in the stagnant pools where the waters never wash,

the tides never reach.

No more than happenstance, maybe,

but we are no dream, we are twilight's children,

never here because we asked.

We are the screams from the next room,

louder than your thoughts,

more urgent than words printed in your books,

screams that you try not to hear,

because we are your shame, your conscience

as you read,

as you write about spirituality

and the evils of moral degradation.

We lurk,

loiter inconveniently in the shadows that you cast,

in the bleakness and miserabilisms

of all the film-noir flicks,

unscripted,

bit-parts beyond the smoke,

beyond where the lamp light fades.

We are what you'll find at the heart of darkness,

resignation,

the fatalism of age,

and we look at life, hollow-eyed, the way old men stare at flies.

It's not your bang or your whimpers

but the silence after the buzz that we fear, if indeed we fear at all.

*

Poor Vivienne, more life than a bag of ferrets,

saw fit to go as a black-shirt to all of his performances,

was it something he said, wrote,

Cable Street, Gerontion, Burbank, Bleistein and all.

And, of course,

friend Ezra played follow Il Duce and Mein Fuhrer, too.

Get thee to a nunnery, did we hear him say to her,

or was it to an asylum,

sectioned and committed, just like us,

to the silence of the cuckoo's nest and he the sensitive poet.

The aristocratic Bertie, he of noble lineage,

had handled the practicalities of sexuality,

to let the poet write,

so kind of the priapic Earl, who also paid the rent.

Good gossip for the 'Bloomsberries',

not for us, though,

we of the lower, vulgar class,

who know nothing

of any French, or the meaning of ménage à trois.

Sad, hapless Vivienne,

her Bury such a long way north from Bloomsbury,

no silk hats or millionaires,

all beer and black-pudding, no books or caviar,

mill-girls on bicycles,

headscarves among the smoking stacks,

just matchstick people and she out-classed,

on the fringe,

vilified, bracketed out,

of an exclusive, aloof coterie of titles,

styles and attitudes, orchestrated, always,

by the vituperative tongue,

the acerbic wit of the odious Mrs Woolf.

The problem of a broken, unconsummated marriage,

just an inconsequential embarrassment,

which we'd never understand,

broken images and all.

Biography, anyway, of no account

in the discourse that they spin, art objectified,

whereby Eliot's waste land becomes a fact,

a truth observed,

that stops us seeing the poet in his poem,

thus there's nothing, it seems, to hide,

no elegy for Verdenal

and the poet never the reality of the waste land he describes.

Strange that a group so avant-garde,

at morality's cutting edge,

should take so much trouble to indict, apportion and obfuscate.

Even us paupers know that every text has a context

and we don't like what we find.

But,

we can see clearly how our entropy,

our decadence,

the vulgarity of our mothers

and their common, uncultured behaviour,

was no more than the subjectivity,

the prejudice of a pretentious and pompous mind.

Clichés and stereotypes come peddled as truth,

with the poet, like Tiresias,

always throbbing between two lives,

and she, like a fledgling in the cuckoo's nest,

sane as you and me,

left to die, a painted shadow in a London lunatic asylum.

*

We know nothing of categorical imperatives

but still carry the idea of freedom in our heads,

to us it's an assumption

and not a gift,

the burden of proof in the taking, never in the giving.

None of us had ever seen a pantomime,

but it's something similar to what we dreamed,

imprisoned children,

a big bad wolf posing as a poet,

and the good fairy, there always, always is,

swinging from strings above a stage

like Tarzan on lianas

across a scratchy, silent film

and we, Mowgli with Bagheera in a dog-eared jungle book.

Best would be Rin Tin Tin

showing a rescue party exactly where we were.

But we know there's no chance of an escape,

no possibility of a rescue,

for as long as Eliot writes the script.

When did he say anything that we would ever want to hear?

Left to him, we'd be another lost generation,

never able to grow up,

our past always surfacing

like a corpse that wouldn't stay buried,

rising inconveniently, like Lazarus, but still in need of crutches.

*

And yet,

one day it came to pass that all the skies were cleared,

the blinds fell down

and all the bells did ring, life not driven by the raids.

Sadly, like broken chairs and empty buckets,

bread and spread for tea,

it was next to meaningless for us,

meant absolutely nothing, when war was all there'd been.

Little Bo Peep, it seemed,

had lost her sheep and didn't know where to find them.

We all knew that and wondered

was there anyone left who even cared enough to look?

She had certainly never found him,

if she'd ever, ever looked.

Perhaps he was like a wound she suffered,

that bled each time they touched,

each time she thought of him,

a cancer she carried and, he, the smoke from her cigarette,

a blemish she had to hide,

behind dark glasses, under a headscarf,

a heavily powdered face.

Or was he something to be ashamed of,

the crooked seam of a stocking, a ladder where it might show.

And he had rarely ever thought of her,

knowing that closeness causes pain,

frightened to invest emotions in unrequited love.

Perhaps she felt the same

and knew, maybe, not to pick the scabs

or fiddle with the wound,

no need to lay the makings of an unsightly, ugly scar.

*

It started with a rash,

gone to a fever, with a head full of bees,

a neck as stiff as boils

and a bed,

clean white sheets, in the tranquillity of a sanitorium,

the lights all too bright.

Days of confusion, nights lost in delirium.

and then a voice of someone, somewhere softly saying,

he's better now, thank God.

And, like a blind pit-pony, left too long in the dark

he's put out to grass,

where cart horses graze,

their eyes benign, their bodies warm and their breath

full of hay, fresh cut grass, soft on his face,

the sensuality he remembered,

the closeness of a mother

in the siren-filled darkness of an under-stair's cupboard.

A farm it was,

with land girls, hair the colour of straw,

who sang as they worked,

'let him go, let him tarry',

a song from a film they'd all just seen.

They were sunshine, they were life,

a beauty he'd never known and knew he'd not forget,

the tender crops, the young sun,

a vision that he'd hold for always,

73

beyond when war's annals had long clouded into night.

Heaven, it seemed, was somewhere deep in the shires,

no sound of silence, no imminent oblivion,

birdsong,

angels in green jumpers who smelt of sunbeams,

a place where we learn the hell of where it is we've been,

the lack of warmth,

the stench of urine and the cold necessities of function.

He'd held the hem of nature, a page-boy in awe,

but he was just a prisoner,

a prisoner on parole, and there was time left to serve.

*

The halls are left as empty,

desks are set, and there are maps, pictures on the walls,

the library dusted and unlocked.

The cellars, deep and dark, where,

when the sirens wailed,

we would slip like Alice, to cower under the raids,

sing songs

and watch the fingered beads of rosaries,

now prepared,

fresh and ready for all their heavy trunks and cases.

We stood and watched them do it,

the stage crew,

waiting, just waiting, as we had all the times before,

waiting for the dawn

for the resurrection game

waiting for something to begin

something to end

waiting always for someone to come,

never knowing who there was,

Rin Tin Tin, Lassie,

Peter Pan, Wendy, or a fairy from a pantomime.

There was carbolic and disinfectant in the toilets,

the smell of cleanliness and care,

a warm and homely welcome

for all the mannered convent girls, safely from the shires.

Back, safely home to the villas that breed gentility,

up west and into Kensington,

Knightsbridge and the like,

out beyond where the bombs fell,

the blue of Park Lane and Mayfair,

the cheery pink of Whitehall and Northumberland Avenue.

While we, we had no possessions,

couldn't even fill our pockets,

were moved out through the Docklands,

the brown of Whitechapel and Old Kent Road,

the cheap end of the board,

where Litvinoff,

learning of the Holocaust,

writes a poem about Eliot's prejudicial view of Jews

and where we tread lightly over their bones.

It was the leaving of bedlam, nodding heads,

rocking beds

and in our waiting moments, we think,

a little like Pooh, maybe,

that because of how it was we feel no sadness in our going.

Out east we went through Hoxton, where Marie was born

and Booth saw no servants,

a tow-path away from Islington,

among the blitzed-out houses, beyond the underground.

Like migrants, their caravans crossing over Europe,

we trailed along the pavements,

no heavy cases,

nothing that would fill a respirator box,

our orphanages gone back to schools, we gone on to care homes.

*

Come the peace and she married again, his mother,

he oblivious, in a care home at the time,

playing in the dust of a back-street yard.

Met him in a betting shop,

a long odds gambler from the last-chance saloon.

Her husband from before,

just terminally infirm, not quite dead it seems.

Much like the Wife of Bath,

busy securing her fifth, the fourth not quite buried.

She knew the wife's prologue, that much was clear,

function and for pleasure hers,

no desires had she for canonisation, sexual martyrdom.

Cassidy and Sundance went south to leave their crimes,

she with him, they did the same.

He with mounting debts,

like a defaulter in fear of Fleet

and she, a Rosie Driffield, a Sally Bowles,

but with no Valerie to sanitize her past,

to hold copyright on her infidelities,

indiscretions

and little derelictions.

So, they sailed into the sunset, like Magwitch transported,

and her child, not so very far from Pip,

left to serve the sentence, the penance for her sins,

an inconvenient little sod, detritus from before.

Strange,

how it's so difficult to crack a brittle heart,

alert, surprise a careless mind,

surely, eventually,

the past must drag back heavy, a secret the weight of hers.

*

Her mother,

like Gertrude with her favours, her husband's bed not cold,

felt she'd been a woman scorned

with her daughter always mindful of her fury.

After twenty years beside the sea,

she went to live in Blackburn with a painter from St Ives,

like Islington in the twenties

where Ferrier sang her songs,

and died in seventy-nine, old as the century,

her worth left to a cat's home, Sally Ann or simply left intestate.

*

We know little of Chablis and Cote du Rhone,

the etiquette,

the practice of red by the bowl

and white by the stem.

What point pretensions when porter is all there is.

Messrs Philby, Blunt, Burgess and Maclean,

Cairncross too, of course,

highly cultural all of them, Oxon, Cantab and the like,

sleeping quietly in the fens,

well, they knew red from white and much preferred the red.

*

Einstein explained the universe,

beyond imagination, anything we knew,

Newton on his head, Eliot's nose out of joint,

82

nineteen twenty-two and all,

but real as the solar-eclipse, that went to prove his case.

So it was with freedom, so difficult to elucidate,

too complex to illuminate.

Tinker Bell and fairy-dust maybe, wings like Peter, perhaps,

some help, possibly, from Rin Tin Tin.

But however it was, freedom came,

curving across the universe,

bending, swerving along the beams of Einstein's stars,

like Larwood's leg-sides at the Oval,

an idea

a mirage

at the speed of light, from a theory to the brilliance of a truth,

the beauty of a Spitfire falling out of the sun.

Jack was nimble,

Jack was quick and Jack jumped over the candle stick,

over the gates and far away,

to a land where the bong tree grows.

And the little dog laughed

to see such sport and the dish ran away with the spoon.

*

No sad Damocles, no pegged out Prometheus,

more Theseus out of the labyrinth,

Oedipus off the mountain,

a train out of a tunnel, fields full of sunshine

and the beauty of solitude, the serenity of the singleton.

Time, maybe, to wipe the slate clean,

mortar dust from shoes,

but tabula rasa, it comes so slow,

and it's a struggle to bury Eliot's corpse,

to carry the weight of freedom,

heavy as the Portland stone of Lutyens' grand sarcophagus.

Urine stained beds and rockets with flaming tails,

the anxiety of silence,

storm lamps deep in cellars,

a waft of paraffin,

times singing London's burning,

and rosaries hung from carbolic-scented hands.

No words, no language, no superlatives enough,

the sweet drift of warm, wet westerlies,

a world breathed into life,

whispers of perfection,

sunshine off the water,

reflections on the ceiling,

windows open wide, staring at forever,

all the way beyond the sun, to the light of Einstein's stars.

But the storm cones rattle along the coast,

red flags fly their warning

and he's been this far before.

The guilt of a survivor, a defector from his class.

And trust, faith, much slower

than the coming of peace, the abatement of a summer storm.

*

Silence is deafening, too long without a word,

and so to Caunterbury they wende,

hand in hand with Dodo to the bricks of the town's asylum,

a character in a novel, like Vivienne, maybe,

seeking help to mend the sick,

a slow pilgrimage to seek the power that creates the flower.

We talk when we're not easy with our thoughts,

so the Prophet says,

resignation perhaps, the fate man was born for,

quietly waiting for it all to end,

dying in a dream,

in the same iron beds, with the same bleak thoughts.

Sheets of blotting paper that Rorschach left behind,

spilt ink and leaky pens,

nothing not squashed in the dark of the blackout,

urine stains and bombsites,

bears, nights and ghoulish nuns, shadows among the beds.

So, back at the Tabard Inn, Dodo wakes him from his sleep,

tells him tales from Chaucer,

the chronicles of Froissart, Crécy and all.

Speaks of her brother, of his polio,

and of limping his way through life,

about her fiancé,

a generation gone to poppies on the Somme,

the poems that they wrote,

a holy place across the water, his name carved in stone.

She shows him the poetry there is in life,

bathes his every vein

in the beauty others saw,

Marvel, Donne, Wordsworth and Blake,

how ugly life's pebbles, how beautiful the clod,

and the love,

the love that Shakespeare invested in the sonnets.

She gives him the daughter of Miss Martha Smoke,

a tortoiseshell kitten named Smut,

who teaches him how to cry,

and a bicycle with Sturmey Archer gears,

Kerouac out on the road,

the whole of life a foreign country, indifference a crime.

And she never,

ever sees life as demeaning as a waste land.

He'd fallen, they both knew that,

badly from the carousel and she was his catcher in the rye.

We had it bad we knew, but Eliot wanted worse,

put us in rats' alley

where the dead men lost their bones,

a scene he borrowed from the Western Front,

he, cosy in Highgate at the time,

teaching a future laureate, the kiddiewinks of his class.

While Marx, screaming from his grave

about the power of the bourgeoisie,

conceded reluctantly that

their ideological domination is never truly complete.

A ray of sunshine warming the philosopher's stone.

So, not wanting to help the poet naturalise

the horrors of the trenches,

as he did the typist's rape,

we bunked off with Geoffrey,

met him back at the Tabard inn,

and walked through hop fields to the Weald,

where they cast the gun-stones for Trafalgar,

the horse-shoes red at Flodden field, the arrows of Poitiers.

Larwood, too, had had concerns and went for good in fifty,

the land of Jardine, Eliot and their class

all left behind because, well,

nothing, we all realised,

ever really grew in Eliot's waste land,

no willow for the bat,

no oaks for Nelson's keels,

we, least of all

and, no matter how we tried,

we couldn't accept our mothers as just vulgar London women.

*

The Poetry of Drouth, a puzzle rather than a poem,

no higher interest than a ship built in a bottle,

and he,

no feeling enough to be a poet, borrows

too much from other men.

Draws heavily on books

for the heat he couldn't derive from life

with a peevish assumption of superiority, underlying it all.

At the bottom, we hear someone say,

he's much like that poor, ridiculous

Mr. Prufrock,

intimidated by all the women who came and went.

And, of course we knew

how discomforted he was with Chaucer,

all that lust and love,

where no-one,

no-one gives a flying fig about problems with a peach,

a prosaic little man,

no capacity for life,

constricted emotional experience,

and you can hardly see the join.

What a shame, what a shame, when he had such a lovely wife.

But yet,

a friend of a friend, of a friend of a friend,

Bloomsbury, Oxbridge and Ivy League,

they came all the way from Munich, appeasers every one,

apologists in velvet jackets,

to the drawing rooms where they lived.

Not an iconoclast among them

and so,

they let a cultural travesty prevail, all too tall above it all.

Honour's voice, though, will never provoke the silent dust,

nor flattery soothe the dull cold ear.

Gray had it right, he spoke for us,

so forget the fourth tempter,

like Fanny, it all leads to no-where but the grave.

In the end, we can't help but wonder,

never mind the peach

and the universe that Einstein fixed,

how he dared presume he was the exception to his drouth.

*

There are no absolutes, no mono-causal reasons,

just lines of thoughts

never really ended,

he says this and she says that,

a subordinate clause for this

another for that,

blame no more than ricochets and tangents,

simple statements mostly left untrue,

where cause and effect lead to nowhere but the garden.

No Bentham, Hobbes or Hume to think things through,

just bit-part players with no Shakespeare to script their lines,

as pigeons fly the paupers' pit

and we,

not obliged to love our mothers, think why should they love us.

*

We'd been buried in the mud of a wasteland

in fields where poppies grow,

felt a sniper's bullet kiss the temple of a poet,

yet we knew nothing of coffee spoons

or anything at all of peaches.

After all,

we were just the paupers,

the ones who filled the pit when Shakespeare filled the Globe.

Slip-sliding out of the sun, hanging in our straps,

we made our Merlins scream,

wrote the poetry of Mitchell's Spitfire across a summer sky, buried ourselves,

in sun-burnished hop fields,

building a heaven in hell's despair. But –

rape, lust, vulgarity, common women, the nymphs departed,

and it's just the naivety of school-boys

defending a moral bankruptcy that really shouldn't be.

He saw a thick, brown fog,

a river that emptied with the tide,

littered mud banks below the walls.

We knew a river, where the charter'd Thames doth flow,

silver in the moonlight,

where the Dornier tracked a city,

saw Guernica on the side of a London bus,

Munch on the doors of the black hackney cabs.

And we had no time,

no time for jingoism, the power of a master morality,

the strutting pomp of an Aryan race,

religious purity,

the triumph of the will,

because we knew that Hitler had only got one ball,

that Goring had two but very, very small.

We were happy being slaves

to kindness, humility, sympathy and empathy,

content with humour, blue, that came all the way from Chaucer.

And yet, he despised us,

despised us from the heights of his ivory tower

with depressive lamentations,

and a woman he failed to please.

The Miller's Tale

and the Wife of Bath, too threatening it seems.

Chaucer though,

with his turds and farts, celebrated his kin,

unashamedly,

we, the common people, Eliot's lower class.

He was one of us, who walked as a pilgrim,

dust upon his feet, and gave expression to our tales,

the richness of our culture.

And they,

one of them the spectre,

the ghost that haunts the other's waste land,

the two of them, as far apart as Canterbury is from Kensington.

*

Mischievous maybe to ask, naïve to only wonder,

but how was he,

he with his gowns, letters and laureate,

after the Holocaust and all,

still at high tables, strolling meadows and playing fields.

They held the keys to veracity and excellence,

his appeasers and apologists,

and he exemplified their views, it seems

and so they gathered

like leucocytes around a wound,

drones around the queen,

an educational elite, cultural clones,

palming off the strikers as they did in twenty-six.

And we hear Miranda's praise for her brave new world,

how beauteous mankind is that has such people in't.

Irony, naivety,

with her not so very far from school, her virtue still intact.

But they, he,

how can any of them possibly know of us,

beyond the dystopias that they tout.

If they think of us at all, it's as carriers, donkeys

to burden with their prejudice,

extras, epsilons, savages to script as they please.

We might be Yossarian scripted in his nose cone,

who learned what we already knew, how

they can do anything to us that we can't stop them doing.

And so it goes, and so it goes,

we hear Billie Pilgrim shrug,

scripted into another wasteland, born of twenty two.

So banish us to your waste land, Malpais and the islands,

but you'll still be the why,

the reason we keep our bowstrings waxed, practise in the butts.

*

He didn't know her either, Marie was not his type,

common little woman, bawdy as the Bard,

a child of Chaucer

who sang how she sits among the cabbages and peas,

and laughingly lampooned

Lord Tennyson's 'Come into the garden, Maud'

with leers, nudges and winks.

He, yet another who knew nothing at all of us,

innuendo and double entendre,

not an aristocratic or puritanical thing, one thinks.

But we, we in the paupers' pit,

the lower class, as we're seen, loved her.

She entertained the troops,

strikers on the picket lines, gave expression to our lives

and she was truly high, as he wrote, in our popular affection.

It may be, after all,

that beer is best, so take care because we haven't spoken yet.

*

She was no Pre-Raphaelite maiden, immortalised on canvas,

though pretty enough to be,

no darling of bohemia, Bloomsbury and all.

No blue stocking from Harvard, Oxon and the like.

She was just a pleb, a Daisy Renton,

an Eva Smith,

the butt for one of Woolf's caustic jibes,

a peasant seen from the heights of Mount Olympus,

just a simple member of a lower class,

vulgar, inelegant, ill-educated and amoral,

despised in the poet's waste land,

one of those who peopled it, used as pawns to make it so.

And, all said and done,

it's impossible to see the bedsits of Ladbroke Grove

and Holland Park

from the gardens of Kensington,

reality, from the window of a drawing-room.

However things are thought, she was never easy to stereotype,

never congruent with a prejudicial line,

always knowing good from evil, the literal from the allegorical.

*

We can't lure back the moving finger

or tear out a single page,

but we can, if we choose, throw the whole book away,

as Esmee tells her priest.

After all, we do have title to our lives.

Even Nietzsche, he of the master morality,

considered such thoughts consoling,

she must have done so too, faltering – sometimes wobbling.

Hers was incremental, a process not a drama,

a character, maybe,

in Hogarth's gin lane, the sad progress of his harlot.

Perhaps, perchance,

Larwood felt the same, a bumping pitch and all,

declaring with a duck on the scoreboard

and nothing in the bank,

just a player when gentlemen, again, held the keys.

So, poor Harold, he kicked over the traces,

pity about the Colonel but sod his vitai lampada.

The aridity of an outback

more congenial than the drought of Eliot's waste land

and a captain's patronising hand,

Sir Pelham and Jardine with the honours, their ashes in the urn.

*

She died in sight of ninety-four, a migrant in another country,

to blush unseen, none to bid goodnight, Irene.

Her life, nervous, unstable and precarious,

Einstein's bicycle just a little too heavy,

always standing on the pedals

pushing hard to keep on moving for fear of falling off

free-wheeling on the downhills

struggling with the climbs,

a virtual one way road, never able to get back home.

Never able to find that innocent, artless girl,

pretty as a picture,

cycling gentle down the ways of those early Islington days,

her Goldengrove

on the margins of a waste land, a spreading conurbation,

before the war,

before she knew what life could do, how hurtful it could be,

so short, it seemed, the craft so long to learn.

No matter, child, the why, sorrow's springs remain the same.

She wanted Chaucer and the sweet-smelling showers of April,

we both did

everyone did

and what we got was Eliot,

who never knew to scatter plenty o'er a smiling land.

They buried her under the name of her birth, a maid

below the dry stone of her life,

with the faith of her fathers long sprinkled from the font.

In her end, it seemed, was her beginning,

and so Eliot might, maybe, have had the last word,

with lipstick and powdered green face,

laughing like the Joker,

like Cabaret's Emcee, down the length of Charing Cross Road.

*

But, as the heart grows older it comes to such sights colder

and it's all, anyway,

from a time now out of mind, things that were and all,

just a child to tell the cautionary tale, that April

might be the cruellest month but the rest, they're not much better.

The Epilogue

Lest we forget those left in the wasteland,

hanging on the wire, waiting while the dark,

chained to railings along Westminster,

the plough and the loom.

For those who filled the paupers' pit,

the trenches

and quietly fill the yards,

mother nature,

she finds a way and time will love her heroes.

Gone to flowers most of them,

the tender crops of spring,

splashed red,

bright across the watered fields of Flanders.

Their tale,

long as history, rehearsed and eulogised,

minstrels and madrigals,

book-people, existential characters,

the players living out their parts.

No paperback fiction, theirs, at literary festivals

and no dystopian fears, come 451.

They trod a pilgrimage severe as Bunyan's,

allegorical, metaphorical,

the celebration of a culture, old as Chaucer,

proud of its pedigree, its veuve, its nerve

to tilt at pomposity, at privilege,

pretentiousness,

at the very core, the pith of conventional wisdom.

The poet's apologies, his guilt-ridden retractions,

no more than Pascal's wager

and, tuppence or not, it will still blow,

the sweet breath of the west wind,

through the upper galleries and all the blinkered minds.

*

Players, actors, that's all we are, in a tapestry

longer than Bayeux.

Surviving knights gone by Binsey Poplars

to the fashionable streets of Bloomsbury,

faded pilgrims, pikestaffs, along the roadsides.

Some by their labours recognised, a pewter pot,

a peasant's tabard,

the shod hoof of a ploughman's dray,

the bobbins of the lace maker

and we the faults, contrived to placate the Deities.

For most of us life's never been a milk run

and our dying so slowly incremental,

never knowing where its thread will end,

the long weave of language,

strands of the vernacular,

a hundred years of poppies in cornfields by the Somme.

Long as the silver chain of the poet's skylark,

our time spent trying to hear its endless notes of glee.

*

Mary from Magdala by the Sea of Galilee,

shaped,

perfected down the centuries,

soothed and washed His feet,

Hogarth's harlot, angelic as the shrimp girl,

rolls back the boulder of the old and sanctifies the new.

And Chaucer, too, his sandals wrung and dusty,

treads the ways, the misty years of history,

immortalised and staring from a Southwark window

redy to wenden

a pilgrymage to Caunterbury,

rolling back the legend, revealing the lessons of the shrine.

Like the clouds that shroud Olympus,

privacy for the Gods,

Valerie's dead hand smothers his many flaws.

While Shakespeare's Juliet, poor thing,

still laments

that what will be, shall be.

And so it shall, but only if the players allow it so.

Best let the sweet smelling showers of April

quench the drought of March,

bathe our every vein,

and have the wheels spin, purr on the avenues,

bumping over history's broken cobble-stones,

rattling the bones of fate,

crossing contour lines,

close on the climbs,

pulses, vital as the racing heart of a foetal child.

There's no felt need of guillotines and tumbrils,

or calls for Byzantium's jewelled beauties,

just the homespun thread of social justice,

the balanced equations of truth,

for we are riding to Utopia

and hear the hallowed notes,

the silver song of the ascending lark,

as we go, blissfully

wheeling our way out of a windswept waste land.

In time, somewhere, our own plaintive tune,

its melancholy strains,

will break our long held reticence,

and fill the silence of the seas, far as the farthest Hebrides.